Usborne Farmyard Tales

SCARECROW'S SECRET

Heather Amery

Illustrated by Stephen Cartwright

Language Consultant: Betty Root

There is a little yellow duck to find on every page.

This is Apple Tree Farm.

This is Mrs. Boot, the farmer. She has two children called Poppy and Sam, and a dog called Rusty.

Mr. Boot is working in the barn.

"What are you doing, Dad?" asks Sam. "I'm tying lots of straw on these poles," says Mr. Boot.

"What is it?"

"You'll soon see," says Dad. "Go and get my old coat from the shed, please. Bring my old hat too."

4

"It's going to be a scarecrow."

Poppy and Sam come back with the coat and hat.
Then they help Mr. Boot put them on the scarecrow.

"He's just like a nice old man."

"I've got some old gloves for him," says Sam.
"Let's call him Mr. Straw," says Poppy.

6

"He's finished now."

"Help me carry him, please, Poppy," says
Mr. Boot. "You bring the spade, Sam."

They all go to the cornfield.

Mr. Boot digs a hole in the field. Then he pushes the pole in so that Mr. Straw stands up.

"He does look real."

"I'm sure Mr. Straw will scare off all the birds,"
says Sam. "Especially the crows," says Poppy.

Mr. Straw is doing a good job.

Every day Mr. Boot, Poppy and Sam look at
Mr. Straw. There are no birds in the cornfield.

"There's Farmer Dray's scarecrow."

"He's no good at all," says Sam. "The birds are eating all the corn and standing on the scarecrow."

"Why is Mr. Straw so good?"

"Sometimes he looks as if he is moving," says Poppy. "His coat goes up and down. It's very odd."

"Let's go and look."

"Let's creep up very quietly," says Sam. And they tiptoe across the cornfield to look at Mr. Straw.

"There's something inside his coat."

"It's moving about," says Poppy. "And it's making a funny noise. What is it?" says Sam.

14

"It's our cat and her kittens."

Carefully they open the coat. There is Whiskers, the cat, and two baby kittens hiding in the straw.

15

"So that's scarecrow's secret."

"Whiskers is helping Mr. Straw to frighten off the birds," says Poppy. "Clever Mr. Straw," says Sam.

First published in 1990 by Usborne Publishing Ltd. Usborne House, 83-85 Saffron Hill, London EC1N 8RT Copyright © Usborne Publishing Ltd. 1995,1990